GETTING STARTED WITH BLENDED LEARNING

How do I integrate online and face-to-face instruction?

William
KIST

 Alexandria, VA USA

Website: www.ascd.org
E-mail: books@ascd.org

www.ascdarias.org

Printed in the United States of America. Cover art © 2015 by ASCD. ASCD publications present a variety of viewpoints. The views expressed or implied in this book should not be interpreted as official positions of the Association.

ASCD LEARN TEACH LEAD® and ASCD ARIAS™ are trademarks owned by ASCD and may not be used without permission. All other referenced trademarks are the property of their respective owners.

PAPERBACK ISBN: 978-1-4166-2119-5   ASCD product #SF115073

Also available as an e-book (see Books in Print for the ISBNs).

Library of Congress Cataloging-in-Publication Data
Kist, William.

 Getting started with blended learning : how do I integrate online and face-to-face instruction? / William Kist.

  pages cm
 Includes bibliographical references.

 ISBN 978-1-4166-2119-5 (pbk. : alk. paper) 1. Blended learning. 2. Educational technology. I. Title.

 LB1028.5.K543 2015

 371.3--dc23   2015028749

24 23 22 21 20 19 18 17 16 15   1 2 3 4 5 6 7 8 9 10

GETTING STARTED WITH BLENDED LEARNING

How do I integrate online and face-to-face instruction?

Want to earn a free ASCD Arias e-book?
Your opinion counts! Please take 2–3 minutes to give
us your feedback on this publication. All survey
respondents will be entered into a drawing to
win an ASCD Arias e-book.

Please visit
www.ascd.org/ariasfeedback

Thank you!

Blended—or Hybrid—Learning

Blended learning is hot! Teachers at all levels are creating lessons, units, and even complete courses that combine traditional face-to-face (F2F) classroom instruction with online components such as video clips, discussion forums, and PowerPoint presentations that students access from home. It's clear that teachers are seeing advantages to both learning arrangements and want their students to benefit from both.

A lot of attention has focused on the growing popularity of online-only courses—and not just at the college level. During the 2013–2014 school year, 16 percent of K–12 students attended a fully online school with no F2F instruction, and 30 states offered fully online statewide schools (Smith, 2014). At least five states *require* each high school graduate to have taken at least one online course (Sheehy, 2012). Institutions of higher education, high schools, and middle schools are seeing how popular online learning is and are trying to catch up with the demand.

Not only are there compelling societal pressures to embrace some form of blended learning, there are also strong pedagogical arguments for doing so. It's evident that many students across the United States are demonstrating the possibilities of online learning outside of school as they curate their own inquiry paths: reading and writing many minutes per day on a screen, writing over 100 text messages per day, and reading and writing hundreds of words per day on social networking sites (Pew Research Center, 2015). It's no wonder teens report being more comfortable writing in online environments than they are in other media (Applebee & Langer, 2013).

Due to a combination of pedagogical, political, technological, and economic factors, more teachers than ever before are confronted with the challenge of moving at least some of their instruction online. And this trend includes me! For the past 15 years, in books and articles, I have chronicled the adventures of teachers all over the world who are using breakthroughs in technology to craft new and exciting teaching strategies and assessments. A few years ago, I found myself in the position of needing to redesign some of my own college classes as hybrid courses. I had to quickly get up to speed but was not sure where to begin! I have gone on to teach hybrid courses almost every semester, including methods courses for undergraduates, research courses for doctoral students, and a first-year English composition course mandated for all majors at my university. I enjoy facilitating blended learning so much that I would find it difficult to go back to completely F2F teaching.

The feedback I have gotten has been impressive. Most of my students go on to become middle school and high school teachers, and I enjoy hearing about the elements of hybrid instruction they have incorporated into their own teaching, with positive outcomes for their own students. For example, one of my former students, Randy Rininger, employs a different hashtag phrase (such as #Mockingbird or #Hamlet) for each piece of literature his high school students study. He has noticed that students tweet on the weekends and at all hours using the hashtag phrase, even when they were studying ancient Greek mythology! Another former student, Angie DiAlesandro, has her high school students take part in a plethora of online activities. She writes, "For a writing-intensive English project, my students create websites using Google Sites. The students use hyperlinks, site maps, image embedding, and other digital tools to complete the project. I use my Google account to leave comments on each individual page to provide feedback. I pair up each student with a partner, and they use GoogleDocs to collaborate on every major writing assignment. Students use the shared documents to provide and receive feedback. This has increased accountability and revision in my classroom."

The purpose of this book is to provide a quick synopsis of the best ideas I have found to make the most of blended instruction. I believe the ideal person to speak to novices about teaching online is someone who was recently a novice himself. It's my hope to provide useful information for those of you who are excited about getting started with hybrid learning as well as those of you who are wary of the whole endeavor. A note about terminology—there are various definitions of hybrid and blended learning. In this book I use them interchangeably to describe any learning experience that is structured to be delivered partially online and partially in an F2F environment.

Although my own hybrid teaching experience has been at the college level, the process of examining course content for ways to match different portions of it with the delivery model that suits it best is essentially the same. The examples and applications included in this book are usable for teachers of grades 4–12 and beyond. I provide some snapshot descriptions of engaging online assignments and assessments to help you navigate the possibilities of teaching and learning in a blended environment. Once you begin, I predict you'll become accustomed and even addicted to the responsive capabilities of a classroom that is 24/7—a classroom that never sleeps.

Where to Begin

When you take up the challenge of moving some of your F2F instruction online, there are several questions that you will need to answer. This section provides these questions as well as some of the answers that I've come up with as I've taught hybrid courses.

- Why do I want to make my lesson, unit, or course a hybrid?
- What hardware and software do I need?
- What is a learning management system, and how do I choose one?
- What are typical experiences that students will have in hybrid environments?

The Rationale for Hybrid Instruction

Even if you are being compelled to hybridize your teaching, you still need to answer some foundational questions about what exactly you want to accomplish. Obviously, you want to meet your particular curriculum goals. So, keeping those in mind, how would you answer the following questions?

- What can students achieve when the learning targets are taught in a blended environment? (Perhaps you might answer that your students will be able to work on assignments that tap into their creativity by making assignments that can be created in a hybrid setting rather than solely in an F2F setting or—gasp—only on paper!)
- What kinds of students can I reach in this new way of teaching—students, perhaps, who are living a great deal of their lives online outside of school? (Perhaps you might answer that you will reach not only students who love spending time online, but also those who are self-directed high-achievers, those who are introverted and like working alone, those who are learning English and might benefit from being able to see demonstrations that can be repeated many times, and those who are groggy and distracted early in the morning but wide awake and ready to learn at 10 p.m.)
- How can I make sure that students who have been successful in F2F environments aren't overwhelmed by this transition to blended learning? (Perhaps you might answer that you need to start slowly, by giving

one online assignment during one grading period, then ramping up the blended component as you and your students become more comfortable teaching and learning in this new way.)

- Why do *I* want to do this?

"Why do I want to do this" is listed last, but it might be the most important question to consider. If your answer is that you want to teach in hybrid fashion because "everyone is doing it" or "because I have to," then you might have missed some of the valuable qualities of this kind of teaching. I hope this book will provide some compelling examples that make the transition to blended instruction something that is seen as inspiring creativity and student engagement. I myself now find it difficult to imagine *not* teaching in a blended environment. Before getting to planning, however, there are more questions that need to be answered, from a technical perspective.

Technical Requirements

The good news is that most teachers who are planning to teach online for the first time already have many of the tools and resources they need. Here are a few basics to think about.

Continuous, reliable Internet access. A reliable Internet connection is a critical component of blended learning. It's what allows students to access assignments, assemble multimedia presentations, and view videos from home. And it's what enables you to check in on the videos and multimedia presentations they are creating, monitor and engage in online discussions, and provide responsive feedback and guidance. Even though you will still be seeing your students in person on a regular if not daily basis, they will be working online outside of your class more often than they would in a traditional F2F classroom. Students who have a question or experience a technical difficulty while attempting to complete an online task are going to quickly become frustrated if they can't get in touch with you. This is not to say that you can't let students know that there are certain times of the day when you will not be responding to e-mail. Setting boundaries is important! But one of the conveniences (and benefits) of this kind of teaching is that it can take place around the clock, and you need to be sure that responding in a timely manner is possible for you.

A laptop with camera and microphone. Some school districts might supply a high-quality laptop or tablet with these features, but if yours doesn't, a personal investment in this kind of equipment might be worth it. The ability to record video and audio will be valuable should you choose to record your own lectures or just to provide audio or even video feedback on your students' work (as is possible within many learning management systems.)

A headset. Along those same lines, it is a good idea to invest in a simple headset that you can purchase at any big box store. These headsets are combination earphones and microphones, and they look like something a sports announcer or an air traffic controller would wear. You will capture better audio when you are recording if you have a microphone that is closer to your mouth.

Learning Management Systems

All online learning must take place within some platform or learning environment, known as a "learning management system" (LMS). Many school districts have purchased a license to an LMS that usually excludes the use of any other LMS. If this is the case for you, you simply need to become familiar with the LMS that's available to you. Most systems have fairly straightforward tutorials that will take you on a tour and explain its features.

Here are the most common LMS features:

- A location for uploading course materials (such as handouts or even streaming video of lectures or other material).
- A location for class discussion (commonly known as a discussion board).
- A location for individual student reflection (aka a blog).
- A location for student work—this could be a space for collaborative or individual work. Some LMSs farm this function out to another provider, like Dropbox, that has room for bigger files.
- A private space for the teacher to give feedback. We'll talk about the specifics of feedback a little later on.

If you do have the freedom to choose which LMS to use, here are some questions to consider:

- Does the LMS include all of the standard features?
- Is the layout of the LMS easy to navigate, or is it difficult to find what you need?

- Is there a "help" function that students can use when they have questions?
- Does the LMS force you into a certain organizational pattern (organizing instruction according to dates, for example, rather than in units or vice versa)?
- Is it easy to make changes to your classroom site if you change your mind about something?
- Is there space to provide private feedback for students?
- Is there room to store large files, or will students have to use Dropbox or some other location outside of the LMS?

If you have a choice over which LMS to use, it's worth remembering that most blog- and wiki-hosting sites, such as Blogger and PBWorks, can fulfill many of the functions of an LMS because you can set aside space for posting class materials and comments. Having your students blog or work on collaborative projects on a wiki is a simple way for you to get started with hybrid teaching if you are tentative about conceptualizing an entire unit or course as a hybrid.

Try not to get too bogged down in choosing an LMS—so many have features that have become universal over the past few years.

What Hybrid Learning Looks Like

Here are the essential kinds of online experiences that students navigate in hybrid classes:

Learning activities. Students respond to an article, chapter of a book, or video you have uploaded to the LMS. Just as in an F2F class, the texts should be chosen with great care. Students will tune out if the video or article is dull or has no clear connection to their learning. This is one of the main challenges of hybrid teaching—figuring out what are failsafe, compelling texts for students to engage with outside of class, when no one is monitoring whether they are really paying attention.

The learning activities tend to fall into four categories.

- **Simple Q&A.** Students answer questions about the texts. Just as in an F2F situation, it's necessary to make sure that these are not just fact-level questions, but rather questions that spark real learning. In an online environment, however, these questions might be asked in a discussion forum so that everyone can share their answers.
- **Posted reflection.** Students reflect, in a more discursive way, on specific elements they have read or viewed. Similar to a blog, this is usually referred to as a post and is longer—perhaps 500–1000 words.
- **Peer response.** Students respond to one or more posts of other students. This could take the form of a fairly formal peer response protocol, or it could be much more informal, with the student just required to say a sentence or two in response to a certain number of other students.
- **Artifact creation.** Students create an online artifact either individually or in groups, such as a video or PowerPoint presentation that they upload to the LMS.

Assessment. Sometimes, students complete an assessment online. It could be as simple as a series of multiple-choice questions or as elaborate as a multimodal composition of some sort.

Many teachers require students to take part in a relatively limited set of activities, but I prefer to vary and expand the kinds of activities my students will do online beyond the basic list. I describe some of these alternative assessments in the next section.

Planning Your Hybrid Instruction

Now comes the fun part: creating your learning experiences and deciding which of them will be online and which will be F2F. Below are some key questions you need to answer, followed by some of my favorite online assignment ideas.

What Are My Learning Objectives and Targets?

Any teacher needs to know the curriculum objectives for a unit or class. In a hybrid environment, this becomes even more crucial; you will need to think very carefully about what aspects of your curriculum might be better served by an F2F environment, and which elements might be more effectively taught online. The first step, before deciding on instructional strategies, is knowing what you want and need to teach! Many school districts and even colleges now provide a curriculum map that includes some underlying goals or standards. Some curriculum maps even break down the standards into discrete learning targets.

If you do not teach in a district (or in a higher education institution) that has such a map, you will want to separate out more specific "learning targets" as shown in the lesson plan format in the Encore. Once you establish your chosen learning targets, you will want to examine these closely to think about certain standards that might lend themselves to online teaching and learning as opposed to F2F learning. What are the qualities of a learning target that might make it most suitable for fitting into a blended environment? Some questions to guide your decision-making process—to help figure out when to use online or F2F instruction—are suggested in the following section.

What's the Best Location for the Learning Strategies I Want to Use?

This is one of the most essential questions when teaching in a hybrid format. When F2F time has been cut in half, it means that the remaining classroom time is precious and must be used wisely.

As you are structuring your lesson, unit, or course, first you will need to think about the assessments that students will have to successfully complete at the end of your unit. This concept of "starting with the end in mind" (Wiggins & McTighe, 2005) suggests that the teacher needs to start with either designing the assessment or becoming familiar with the pre-existing district or school assessment. Ideally, the assessments will gather together the skills and understandings that students should acquire by the unit's end.

The good news for teachers who are interested in implementing blended learning is that, at the K–12 levels, both the PARCC and Smarter Balanced assessments (which are designed to align with the Common Core State Standards) have at least some assessment items that must be taken in screen-based environments. Both also feature multi-step assessment items that are similar to many of the kinds of tasks you will probably want to include within your hybrid space and also work well for gathering formative assessment data. States that have not adopted the Common Core feature similarly formatted questions on their high-stakes exams. So, as you think about the standardized tests for which you are held accountable, you will probably want to include some items in your online space that resemble the screen-based items on your particular standardized test. This has the double advantage of preparing students for the format of the assessment and addressing the content in the way any well-designed learning activity should.

As you begin to sort your desired instructional strategies into two categories—those best taught in an F2F environment and those best taught online—keep an open mind. A surprising number of the instructional strategies you might assume require an F2F environment actually work even better in an online one. For example, while one might think that an F2F setting would be a given for objectives and assessments related to public speaking, students could also record themselves performing a speech and to upload it to the classroom LMS (or to YouTube or Vimeo). Another possible assessment to consider administering online is to ask students to create a presentation in the form of a PowerPoint or Prezi that includes voice-over narration and that summarizes a complex concept. Assessing in an online environment also opens up the possibility of an arts-based assessment, such as asking students to represent their learning in the form of an animated diagram or graphic design.

As you consider how to use your F2F time vs. your online instructional space, consider the following questions to guide your decision making.

Is there any reason this instructional strategy must be done in an F2F meeting? For instance, I do an activity with my students in which we collaboratively build a rubric to assess the ideal chocolate chip cookie. Then we taste five different chocolate chip cookies and use the rubric to determine how the various cookies rate. The strategy is designed to help students understand the rationale for using rubrics: to ensure that students and teachers are on the same wavelength regarding an assignment's expectations for quality. Obviously, there is no way that I can ask my students to taste cookies online. We must be together in person to taste the cookies and to hash out what criteria to use when assessing a chocolate chip cookie. Similarly, in a science class, some lab experiments are impossible to do online; students need access to equipment and materials that they cannot access outside of school. Many classroom teachers across disciplines like to use drama games and activities, including choral speaking and acting out scenes, to help students process content. These, also, are best reserved for F2F sessions. In addition, providing coaching for students who are behind or do not understand the material can certainly be done online, but there are many situations when it might be necessary to have some F2F give-and-take between a teacher and student.

Does the standard being taught specifically mention "alternative" media? Several standards involve some aspect of being able to read and write online or with non-print media. For example, the following standard from the Common Core (Reading Information Text, Grades 11-12, #7) mentions comparing different media texts: "Integrate and evaluate multiple sources of information presented in diverse formats and media (e.g., visually, quantitatively, as well as in words) in order to address a question or solve a problem." Standards that explicitly mention multimedia texts certainly lend themselves to being assessed and practiced in an online space.

Is the learning target best practiced and assessed over an extended period of time? Complicated multi-step performance assessments are sometimes difficult to administer within the constraints of an instructional period, some of which are as short as 40 minutes. Allowing students to work on projects outside of the school day enables assignments and assessments that don't have to be rushed. One example is asking the students to shoot and edit a video clip or compile data from soil samples taken over a period of days. Being able to transfer some of these kinds of complex tasks to an environment in which they can be completed over a number of days will open up more possibilities for authentic assessment.

Is memorization necessary to demonstrate learning? This issue can be divisive in that there is great difference of opinion among educators regarding just how essential memorization is to learning. If you believe that a curriculum learning target necessitates that students memorize some specific facts or functions, then placing an assignment or assessment online might not be the best choice, in that students are going to be able to look up the answers on the Internet.

How much can the learning target be practiced and assessed without the teacher's presence? In a blended learning activity, the teacher is not immediately there. Yes, the teacher can be "present" via pre-recorded online tutorials, but some learning targets, such as factoring a polynomial or working through the analysis of a primary source document, might be best practiced within an F2F setting in which the teacher can demonstrate and then moderate and "think-aloud" the practice.

What Online Learning Strategies Can I Use?

Discussion questions and shared responses. As discussed earlier, one of the most commonly used strategies in online learning is to have students read an article or watch a video and then answer discussion questions about what they've read or seen. This is why so many LMSs have similar features. The questions are usually (but not always) answered within some kind of discussion board, so that the class can see everyone's answers.

While there is certainly nothing wrong with having students answer questions about a text they've read, teachers who rely exclusively on this strategy in online settings are underutilizing the online teaching environment just as teachers who excessively lecture are underutilizing the F2F learning environment. It's important to remember that not every learning task needs to be accomplished within the LMS. Here are some online strategies that I have used over the years or that I've seen others use.

Scavenger hunts (aka "webquests"). This is probably one of the oldest online teaching strategies—simply have students go to a designated website and find information or perform tasks that can only be accomplished at that site. Students can post their answers to the discussion board or on their own blog or wiki page. This is an excellent pre-reading strategy to get students thinking about the essential questions for the unit. Structuring your webquests around blogs is also a great way to introduce their educational uses. For example, if you are teaching a unit on oceanography, find a few blogs written by oceanographers and assign your students to go to these blogs and leave a comment. Another challenge of the webquest might be for each student to find another blog that is linked to one of the first blogs you have found. These blogs could become part of the assigned reading for the class, with students posting responses on the class discussion board.

Annotating a text. Ask students to take a section of any text you are studying and annotate it. This can be done any number of ways, from simply asking them to type the text into a word document and embed a certain number of hyperlinks, to having them use an app such as Evernote. Applications such as Thinglink and VoiceThread allow students to make voice and word-based comments in reaction to multi-modal texts. This is a good assignment with material that students don't find engaging. For example, taking a section of a history textbook that deals with a complicated portion of the Revolutionary War or Civil War, and asking students to embed a certain number of hyperlinks into that text, can get students to slow down and make connections between what they are reading and the locations where the battles take place just through the act of hyperlinking.

Annotating a peer's text. An extension of the previous idea is having students annotate each other's text. Google Classroom allows teachers and students to make audio files (MP3) in response to texts. I've found that students seem much more liberated to give peer responses when working online rather than in an F2F environment. (Not always in a good way; more will be said about establishing group norms in the next section.)

Listening to virtual guest speakers. Finding experts to work with your students is surprisingly easy. Invite the expert to do a live video stream with students. Another option is to ask the expert to take part in a Google hangout or a Twitter discussion using a certain hashtag. Or it might be more convenient for your expert to pre-record a presentation that students may access at a certain time.

Taking or creating virtual field trips. Apps such as Google Earth and MapQuest allow you to take virtual field trips. Many places of study, from the Parthenon to the Louvre, offer virtual tours that students can take. But in addition to taking preexisting virtual field trips, consider assigning students to create their own virtual field trips using images they obtain from Google Earth. This virtual field trip could also be tied to your virtual guest speaker—for example, assign students to take a virtual field trip to the guest speaker's place of work. Teams can collaborate on these field trips to talk about the university or workplace of your expert speaker. This idea came from Garth Holman, social studies teacher at Beachwood Middle School in Ohio. Holman's seventh graders had an F2F visit from a curator from a museum in Paris. When she returned to France, the students used Google Earth to pinpoint her museum and even plot her trip to and from work (because she was willing to provide them with the name of the street where she lives). Students were able to learn not only about the ancient civilizations she studies, but also the world of a modern day museum curator.

Live tweeting. Using hashtag phrases on Twitter can make for instant meet-ups for students. If you are fortunate to be teaching current events during some momentous historic event, you can assign students to "live tweet" during the event. You can easily monitor their tweets afterward by assigning them to use a certain hashtag and searching for that hashtag after the event. They can also archive the discussion in Storify and present to the teacher for grading. Live tweeting can also be used during an F2F session in which students might tweet out their solution to a math problem or to any topic of discussion. Outside of the F2F session, you could assign students to live tweet during a candidates' debate or another ongoing current event.

Creating multi-modal texts. Assigning students to create multi-modal texts is a great use of online spaces. Students could make videos or podcasts or create artifacts in such spaces as Glogster, VoiceThread, PowToon, and Popcorn Maker. There are many opportunities for collaborating within the hybrid space—students can divide up parts of the assignment and work on them individually until putting them together upon submission. This kind of assignment has long been assigned in F2F environments—for example, assigning students to make a diorama of the Alamo or a dinosaur face-off. But by using the available online tools, students can create an animation of a scientific process, a poem, or the stylistic progressions of a visual artist. I have frequently asked students to create an abstract video representation of a book using MovieMaker or iMovie. A similar assignment is to ask students to make a book trailer—most authors now have trailers (video previews) that can be used as models for this assignment.

Taking part in communities outside the LMS. Any topic of study, from the Civil War to the migratory patterns of whales, has a community of bloggers or some presence within social media. If you are an English teacher, assign students to open a GoodReads account and post a certain number of reviews of books. (There is also GoodFilms for discussing films.) You or the students can research the popular blogs, Twitter feeds, and Facebook groups within a certain area of interest. Have students provide proof of their participation by copying and pasting posts they have made into their discussion board or page.

Curating learning. Ask students to make use of existing platforms to create and monitor their own learning. New technology tools allow students to be able to collect and, in effect, curate all of the texts and learning experiences they have across disciplines and media (Beach, Anson, Breuch, & Reynolds, 2014). This kind of curation can be accomplished within your LMS, within a blog that the student is assigned to keep, or using an app such as Evernote or Mahara. One of the most commonly used examples of this kind of assignment is to ask students to create a YouTube channel in which the student curates video clips found within the site that relate to a particular topic or learning focus. Assign each student a certain element of the topic and then post a link to the video channel so that the entire class can peruse the collected videos. No matter what is being studied, there are video clips on YouTube that relate to that topic. Assigning students to curate their learning allows them to demonstrate expertise on a certain aspect of what is being studied. This assignment can also be accomplished with music. Ask students to curate a playlist within Spotify or iTunes that relates to the topic.

Writing a discipline-based memoir. This assignment asks students to remember the first time they thought about science or social studies or whatever the subject or focus

(Kist, 2010). This kind of memoir assignment can be a great way to start the class or hybrid experience. By remembering and writing about the first time they encountered something in nature, a past trip to a historical site, or the first time they solved a real-world math problem, students can jumpstart an inquiry project. The assignment functions as a pre-writing activity that can help students see how many facets of a subject are available for study and further inquiry. They can present this memoir online as a simple PowerPoint, iMovie, or VoiceThread.

Assembling text sets. A seemingly simple task, but one that can grow quite far-reaching, is to ask students to assemble various texts that relate to the theme being studied. This is often referred to as assembling a text set and could include all kinds of media related to the topic of focus—books, films, graphic novels, poems, or songs. By collecting texts from different media related to a certain topic, students see the larger thematic connections between multiple texts—this assignment helps students to focus on higher-level considerations of what is being studied rather than simple fact-level recounting (Pytash, Batchelor, Kist, & Srsen, 2014).

Creating a multimedia vocabulary notebook. Ask students to keep an online vocabulary notebook with a separate page for each word. Students assemble images, sounds, and video clips that elaborate on the vocabulary words. In some cases, such as when studying something in science, the picture accompanying the word can be of the actual object or process being described. In other instances, perhaps in social studies or English, the picture might be more of an abstract representation of the word being studied. In fact, the images that students choose are sometimes so tangentially linked to the word that this assignment can provoke some interesting conversation on the discussion board, as peers weigh in on why the picture chosen is or is not appropriate.

How Should I Organize My Online Experience?

As I prepared to teach hybrid courses, I also began to study others' hybrid spaces. One of the people I reached out to was my colleague at Kent State University, Melanie Kidder-Brown, who has taught online courses for years. Melanie's site seemed extremely easy to use and understand. Her online courses are completely organized by week, with four components per week: "What to Do," "What to Read and/or Watch," "What to Print Off," and "Things to Start Thinking About (Any assignments that will be due within the next two weeks)." It's very clear to the students that there will be these four components every week.

Some instructors organize their online spaces by units, but, like Melanie, I find sticking with the calendar as my organizer works for me. Also, I don't upload all of my assignments weeks in advance because I like to have some flexibility over what I add or take away, based on the needs of my students. Some teachers are worried that online learning is too unstructured and loose, so they feel they must enforce rigid deadlines and practices. Of course, there should be some repeating structure—I try to make sure there is a similar amount of work each week so that students know what to expect. But if you upload many assignments and assessments into the future, complete with due dates, you run the risk of locking yourself into a plan that is not student-centered. When such an online plan doesn't seem to be working, there are only two choices. The teacher can change the due date (which sometimes leads to student confusion and makes you very unpopular with students who have already completed the assignment). Or the teacher can go through with the published plan and force the class in lockstep through the learning activities just to keep on schedule. I have been most happy in hybrid teaching when I have not distributed my plan too far into the future, allowing me to upload a last-minute text and accompanying questions or make a revision to an assignment based on something that occurred in my F2F sessions.

Finally, make sure that what is posted online is well organized and uncluttered. You can troubleshoot some of the questions and directions on assignments in person, but you want to make sure that your activities are as clear and comprehensible as possible. If you are constantly being asked to clarify your online activities, you will miss out on the wonderful untethered quality of blended instruction.

How Should I Structure Online Discussions?

Although discussion boards tend to dominate online learning environments, it's worth thinking about structuring your online experiences around a blog or a wiki. Wikis are essentially websites that can be created with multiple pages (the most famous example is, of course, Wikipedia, an online encyclopedia written and edited by volunteers). There are several sites available for hosting wikis, including PBWorks and Wikispaces. The nice thing about setting up a wiki is that it can be completely private, and it can host student work, including blogs. Each student in your class could have his or her own page on the class wiki, where students can blog or post any work that is assigned. An advantage to using a blog system, whether it's located within a wiki or not, is that it allows space for students to write lengthier posts and delve more deeply into a topic. If there a research component to the class, the blog or wiki can become the venue for research notes and citations. Discussion boards tend to favor shorter posts and allow for threaded discussions with students quickly able to see the hot topics and comment on them. Of course, there is no reason why you can't have both a discussion board and a blog within your hybrid class.

I have used a class wiki when the designated LMS was not user friendly for either myself or my students or because it didn't include a feature that I needed. Using a wiki means that I, as the instructor, get to structure the environment precisely the way I want to. Students have more freedom as well, as they have their own pages and blogs. Each student can simply go to that page and write a post. Both of the popular wiki-hosting sites (PBWorks and Wikispaces) allow students to comment on each other's pages, so that you can simply go to each student's page and read the student's posts and the comments.

Will Discussions Be Synchronous or Asynchronous?

It is technically possible, in many cases, to ask your students to log in to your LMS at a certain time so that you can all participate in a discussion together. In a hybrid course, this probably won't be necessary because you will be meeting F2F. To date, I have never done synchronous discussions within a hybrid course. Forcing students to log in at a certain time defeats one of the main purposes for creating a blended experience: the freedom it allows students to do at least some coursework at any time it's convenient for them.

How Do I Assess in a Hybrid Class?

In a hybrid environment you can organize your class so that some major assessments will be administered during the F2F portion of the class. This could include, of course, paper-and-pencil tests as well as presentations that are delivered in front of a class.

However, one of the advantages of teaching online is that you are able to set up performance tasks with multiple steps the same way they will be delivered to students on standardized tests. Students will be expected to look at texts online, draft an outline, and then write an essay response to the text. All of this will be done on a computer, so your students have the opportunity to practice this essential skill of completing several steps in an online environment. Many of the tasks described above can easily function as performance assessments to determine whether students have the ability to perform the curriculum objective.

Many teachers use some kind of "exit slip" at the end of a traditional F2F class to see whether there is understanding and how the data can inform the next instruction. Gathering formative assessment data within hybrid settings works the same way, but never has it been so quick and easy to find out what (if anything) your students have learned. Just by having students post a quick answer to a question, such as "What are the six conjugations of the imperfect tense of the verb 'aller'?" or "How would you solve the following equation?" allows the teacher to see very quickly which students are grasping the material and which are not. Of course, the main point of collecting formative assessment data is to help you form future instruction. Be prepared to act on what the data is showing you about what your students know and what they can do.

When collecting formative assessment data, don't forget that you can use online venues other than your LMS to gather information. For example, you can pose a question at the end of an online activity that they have to answer on Twitter. By using the hashtag phrase, you can collect students' answers later. Or you could do an online version of a common F2F debriefing activity that asks students to write one or more things learned during the lesson or any questions on the back of an index card (Silberman, 1996). When doing this online, students can post in the LMS or on Twitter what they have learned and synthesize what other students have posted. (If doing this F2F, students circulate the room and exchange cards with a certain number of students and then try to remember trends in what others have written.)

Getting students to think about the big picture of what their peers have learned (or haven't learned) can sometimes help them to realize gaps in their own knowledge. I've found over the years that students of all ages seem to be much more perceptive about others' flaws and virtues than they are about their own.

Tips for Conducting and Evaluating Your Hybrid Class

This section provides suggestions for helping you conduct the teaching of your hybrid course—including how to gather feedback from your students so that you can improve the design of your next hybrid course. Some of these tips are based on my own experiences, and some are from colleagues who have taught in blended environments for years.

Establish Some Group Norms

Most teachers conduct their classes within some established overarching school code of behavior, but sometimes these rules do not include online behavior, and it's important to be specific about this. One of the benefits of teaching a hybrid class is that you can talk about some of these "netiquette" issues when together in person—these guidelines are not only listed in your syllabus or other online materials but also reinforced in person. Some of the following group norms are ones that I and some of my middle school and high school colleagues have established when conducting a hybrid class:

- No hate speech may be used during F2F class sessions, in discussion boards, or in response to anyone's work.
- Personal concerns about an assignment or assessment need to be addressed to the teacher directly, not on a discussion board.
- When collaborating with others, each person needs to fulfill expectations in a timely and complete way. If some life event happens that prevents you from completing an assigned task, you need to communicate promptly to the group your inability to complete the task and copy the teacher if you are communicating this via e-mail.
- Make sure that you come prepared and on time to F2F classes—our F2F time together is valuable. Showing up unprepared or late, or not showing up at all will seriously damage your ability to learn.

One of my former graduate students, Nora Faul, a mathematics teacher at Hudson High School, in Hudson, Ohio makes the point that many LMSs allow for keeping close tabs on student activity, serving as extra insurance that group norms are maintained. She uses Educreations to produce and share videos with her math classes. "Each student is given a password for his or her class," Nora says. "They must log in to Educreations the first night of school. I count that logging in as a three-point homework grade.

When the students are assigned a video, they are given an entrance ticket on the following day. There will also sometimes be group work in class based on what they've learned from the videos. This helps students to fine-tune the more difficult concepts." Some LMSs will send an e-mail to the teacher each time a student posts something, allowing for the teacher to immediately remove a comment that is inappropriate. Many organizations provide guidelines for staying safe in general when surfing the Internet outside of the LMS; see, for example, Cyberwise.org and SafeKids.com.

In addition, Nora has strongly worded homework and attendance policies. When a course takes place partially online, teachers need to be very clear about when assignments are due and how they are to be submitted. The teacher is not going to be present, in person, to remind the students to turn in their homework. The burden is more clearly placed on the students to remember and, so, these deadlines must be clearly stated. When teaching blended courses at the college level, every one of the F2F meetings becomes more important. There need to be penalties for excessive absences. Include an explicit statement about whose responsibility it is to secure make-up work and very clear wording about when or if late work will be accepted.

Set Aside Time for Everyone to Introduce Themselves Online

Within a hybrid class, you will get to know your students and they will get to know each other during your F2F sessions, but I also think it's worthwhile to make one of your early online assignments involve brief introductions. This is especially useful when assigning online group projects. One of my favorite icebreakers is called "Group Resume" (Silberman, 1996) in which each person in the group provides information about talents, hobbies, travel, family, and various accomplishments. Each individual's contribution is noted and preserved in a list for each group, and is then combined in an online space with those of classmates to form a composite portrait of the strengths and accomplishments of the entire group—the group's resume. Taking advantage of the multi-modality of being online, you could assign students to make a video introduction of themselves or produce a podcast or piece of music that allows students to get to know each other in this new way. Just throwing out a simple get-to-know-you question might be all you need to get students interacting with each other. The discipline-based memoir assignment mentioned earlier can function as this kind of introductory activity. At the same time they are uploading their introductions or taking part in the Group Resume, they are also practicing with the unique elements of your LMS's interface.

Be Ready to Help Students with the Technical Requirements

It might surprise you just how much help your students might need to navigate the online portion of your hybrid experience. We tend to think of our students as digital natives who are able to master any new technology quickly, but I have found that many young people need just as much explanation as older students or adults when it comes to navigating a hybrid learning experience. Again, one of the benefits of blended learning is that during F2F time, I can go over in person how to post a comment to the discussion board, how and where to deposit student work, and how and where to blog. And I can explain exactly what needs to be done with a certain assignment or assessment. This is information is also present online, but it helps to have the additional ability to explain technical issues in person.

Most of the online activities I do beyond the LMS (as described earlier) can go more smoothly with some in-person explanation or modeling by me or one of the students. For example, I've been surprised how many of my students have never used the hashtag feature of Twitter. I've also noticed that I need to demonstrate features of track changes in Microsoft Word (or the analogous features within Google Classroom or the LMS) that allow me to respond to student work electronically. I like to have my students comment on each other's work using track changes. If I am using Google Classroom as my LMS, students might not know the difference between a "Suggestion" and a "Comment." Don't assume that students know these terms and how they work within your LMS. Explaining them in person and being ready to respond with questions via e-mail will help lower the frustration levels of your students and allow them to concentrate on the task at hand.

Make Sure You Stay on Top of E-Mail

While you will see your students in F2F sessions, it is still important to keep on top of your e-mail. Technical frustrations can arise quickly when students are trying a new assignment for the first time. Students really appreciate it when they discover that the instructor is responsive to student inquiries. Make sure you are in a situation where you are able to stay on top of your e-mail. Most e-mail programs, such as Outlook, give you the ability to funnel e-mail into various folders that you set up, so you might want to set one up specifically for e-mails related to your hybrid class. I prefer to act on each e-mail as it arrives.

However, the e-mail onslaught can get overwhelming, particularly when due dates for assignments are near. Again, it is very important for the teacher to make sure that deadlines are clearly stated and embedded in several locations within the assignment description and, perhaps, in a timeline or syllabus that is always available. To cope with the e-mail barrage, some teachers prefer to tell students that there are only certain times of the day when they will be available for "office hours." This helps cut down on confusion or frustration on the part of the student if there is a delay in the teacher's response. The student can clearly see when the teacher is "off duty." Of course, the drawback of setting these kinds of office hours, is that the teacher must make every attempt to be online during the posted office hours. This kind of rigidity of hours might not be attractive. For myself, I choose to answer e-mail whenever it comes in (within a few hours, if I can). I would rather deal with a steady trickle of e-mail throughout the day than a stuffed inbox when it comes time for my "office hours." Your e-mail habits are yours and should suit your needs as much as possible. Just don't forget to communicate your preferences with your students.

Be Nimble

One of the great things about teaching in a hybrid environment is that you can respond instantly to an event or innovation and weave it into your course. F2F teachers have always had the ability to be quick on their feet, but in a hybrid environment, you can reach out to your students immediately and perhaps even ask them to complete an online task before the next F2F meeting. (Of course, as mentioned earlier, you can only be nimble if you haven't locked yourself into an already published timeline of planned-out activities!) I can point to several examples of last-minute opportunities that I've been able to capitalize on over the years, often between F2F sessions. In other words, if I hadn't had the ability to reach out to students and ask them to perform some task between F2F sessions, I would have lost a teachable moment. A few years ago, one of my students showed me the project called FreeRice.com, which is a vocabulary-building online game that also has a charitable goal. For each vocabulary question the online viewer answers correctly, 10 grains of rice are donated to the World Food Programme. Though I heard about this site mid-course, it was something I could easily weave into some of my next week's activities. Many of these kinds of projects achieve a critical mass overnight, so it helps to be observant and quick in response.

Another site I first heard out about from a student was Vine.co, which is a social networking site that allows users to post videos that are 6.5 seconds long. I made it one of the options for student reflections. Over the years, I've been able to respond to last-minute epiphanies and put together quick online applications that might have been difficult to take advantage of in an exclusively F2F class. One such recent discovery has been HitRECord, a site created by actor Joseph Gordon-Levitt that allows anyone older than 13 to collaborate on various art works. Another example of a current event was Anne Teresa de Keersmaeker's challenge for people to upload videos of themselves dancing a piece of her choreography. Almost 1,500 people worldwide responded to it instantly. Last year, I heard an excerpt from President Obama in which he used pathos, ethos, and logos in one relatively brief sound bite. I was able to upload the clip of this appearance to my LMS and ask students to view it before coming to class so that we didn't have to take class time to view it.

Of course, social studies and science teachers often have the chance to point students to current events, whether it might be a combat situation or an earthquake or sudden eruption of a volcano. Being able to weave such occurrences into online tasks at the last minute helps make your class fresh and relevant to students. And more importantly, it makes the learning more authentic and parallel to the online ways we interact with the world.

Be Careful Not to Crowd Your Online Space

While it's tempting to find all sorts of links and texts for your students, one of the criticisms you might receive from students is that the class is too crowded and complex and that it involves too much work. We teachers tend to be passionate about our subjects and get excited when we find the latest link or multimodal text related to our units of study, but too many texts and tasks in the online portion of the class may overwhelm students. We have to be careful not to be virtual hoarders, cramming every relevant YouTube clip and hyperlink from our own personal stashes.

I also think that sometimes teachers feel that online teaching is somehow inferior to fully F2F classes, and, so, they overcompensate by being rigorous in their online expectations. But in most cases, less is more. Many online classroom spaces seem overly busy and overwhelming to navigate—with multiple folders and overlapping directions that students must open and make sense of. I urge any teacher beginning to teach a hybrid unit or class to scale back at first on the number of online tasks and be responsive to student feedback on a regular basis. This is another reason for not locking in to a rigid class outline for an entire semester, especially when teaching a hybrid unit or class for the first time. Ask your students frequently how the class or learning experience is going, and they will tell you.

Finally, especially if this is the first time you have taught in a hybrid environment, consider asking a teacher with more online teaching experience to evaluate your class design, including your assignments and assessments. For more specific feedback, ask your colleague to observe an F2F lesson and give feedback about whether the strategies you are using in the classroom integrate well with the online activities you designed for the topic of that lesson. You might also ask to observe one or more of her classes.

Listen to What Students Are Telling You About Your Teaching

Waiting until the end of the course or learning experience (as is commonly done at the college level) to ask students to fill out formal evaluations is too late. You need to ask some evaluative questions throughout your hybrid teaching experience, especially if this is the first time you have taught in blended fashion. Below are some sample questions.

- What parts of this class worked well online? Would some of the activities have worked better in class?
- Did the classroom activities and online activities seem to go together? Did you feel like you were taking one course or two separate ones?
- Did you prefer the classroom or online part of the course?
- Do you feel that this class involved too much work, just the right amount of work, or not enough work?
- Did the assignments seem clear to you? Did you have the information that you needed? Please explain your answer.
- If you used e-mail to ask questions, did you get the answers you needed to complete the assignment on time?
- Would you want to take this course without the online part? Explain your answer.

- Would you want to take this class fully online, without any classroom meetings? Explain your answer.
- What did you like about the LMS? What did you not like?
- Overall, what have you learned from this class?
- What would you have liked to learn that you have not?

Checking in with students doesn't have to be excessively formal. Ask students occasionally how things are going, and ask them specifically to comment on the online and F2F aspects of the learning. I've found that students will give quite elaborate feedback within an online setting, especially if you demonstrate that you are open to feedback and not going to penalize them for giving you their honest opinions. Be prepared to be hurt. But the feedback is invaluable: I've been able to alter online portions of assignments or move an online activity into an F2F session based on feedback I've received from students in the past.

Do the Online Assignments First Yourself

This is also similar to an evaluative activity you might do in a traditional class, but is probably more important when giving online assignments. When doing the assignment yourself, you may discover a missing direction or a technological glitch what will frustrate your students. You might also discover some potentially tricky portions of the task that you might want to model for students. During one of your F2F sessions, you could do a think-aloud of your own process of navigating some of the challenging parts of the assignment (Afflerbach & Johnston, 1984). The think-aloud strategy can be particularly useful for English language learners (McKeown & Gentilucci, 2007).

* * *

The suggestions in this section and in this entire book come from my own hybrid teaching and from teachers I've admired and written about. Now, even when I teach a course that is completely F2F, I still have some kind of online space for the class—there are just too many things I want my students to see and to do that can only be done online and, really, that shouldn't be done during our F2F time. It's difficult to think of a work or school or entertainment experience we have today that isn't a blend in some way of virtual and F2F experiences. It makes sense that so many teachers are finding the way to this kind of teaching!

To give your feedback on this publication and be entered into a drawing for a free ASCD Arias e-book, please visit
www.ascd.org/ariasfeedback

ENCORE

CHECKLIST FOR STARTING YOUR HYBRID LEARNING EXPERIENCE

☐ **Come up with a rationale for why you want to include hybrid learning experiences.** If it's just because everyone else is doing it, that's probably not enough of a rationale!

☐ **Make sure you have the technology in place both for yourself and for your students.** Broadband Internet access for both you and your students is a must.

☐ **Make sure you have a Learning Management (LMS) System in place.** These are LMSs that I have often encountered over my years of teaching hybrid classes and talking to those who teach hybrids. Each of these offer the standard features of online learning experiences, such as providing space for uploading your own materials, and space for posting of student responses, work, and peer critiques.

- Blackboard
- Canvas
- Collaborize Classroom
- Educreations
- Eli Review
- Google Classroom
- Moodle
- Ning

- Open Class
- Schoology
- Sophia
- The Writing Studio (Writing.colostate.edu)

In addition, most sites that have the capability of hosting blogs also offer many of the features of LMSs.

- Blogger (part of Google)
- Blog.com
- LiveJournal
- Typepad
- WordPress

The two dominant wiki-hosting sites also provide complete course management systems when creating a wiki.

- Wikispaces
- PBWorks

☐ **Take time to scope out which of your learning targets lend themselves to blended learning.** Some of the standards that mention using a variety of media are obvious ones to use at the beginning.

☐ **Choose online learning strategies.** There are many sources for online and blended activities that have already been successfully used by others, including the options listed below.

Websites

- www.ck12.org (STEM only)
- www.hybridpedagogy.com
- http://interact-simulations.com
- www.icivics.org
- www.khanacademy.org
- www.engageny.org
- www.merlot.org
- www.mvlri.org
- http://ocw.mit.edu/index.htm
- http://ctl.iupui.edu/OnlineTeaching

Print resources

Baldino, S. (2014). The classroom blog: Enhancing critical thinking, substantive discussion, and appropriate online interaction. *Voices from the Middle*, *22*(2), 29–33.

Boettcher, J. V., & Conrad, R. M. (2010). *The online teaching survival guide: Simple and practical pedagogical tips*. San Francisco, CA: Jossey-Bass.

Conrad, R. M., & Donaldson, J. A. (2011). *Engaging the online learner: Activities and resources for creative instruction* (Updated ed.). San Francisco, CA: Jossey-Bass.

Fassbender, W. J., & Lucier, J. A. (2014). Equalizing the teacher-to-student ratio through technology: A new perspective on the role of blended learning. *Voices from the Middle*, *22*(2), 21–28.

Ferdig, R. E., & Kennedy, K. (Eds.). (2014). *Handbook of research on K–12 online and blended learning.* Pittsburgh, PA: ETC Press. Retrieved at: http://press.etc.cmu.edu/content/handbook-research-k-12-online-and-blended-learning-0

Garrison, D. R. (2011). *E-learning in the 21st century: A framework for research and practice* (2nd ed.). New York: Routledge.

Gonzalez, A. (2014). Strategies to get started with blended learning. *Voices from the Middle*, *22*(2), 34–38.

Hirumi, A. (Ed.). (2014). *Grounded designs for online and hybrid learning: Design fundamentals.* Eugene, OR: ISTE.

Ko, S., & Rossen, S. (in press). *Teaching online: A practical guide* (4th ed.). New York: Routledge.

Moss, B. (2014). Blended learning resources for middle grade teachers. *Voices from the Middle, 22*(2), 10–12.

Thormann, J., & Zimmerman, I. K. (2012). *The complete step-by-step guide to designing and teaching online courses.* New York: Teachers College Press.

Warnock, S. (2009). *Teaching writing online: How and why.* Urbana, IL: NCTE.

☐ **Make sure you have planned your blended learning experiences well.** Consider using the lesson plan format below.

GRADE LEVEL:

STANDARD STATEMENT (Copy exact wording from Common Core State Standards or your district's curriculum):

LEARNING TARGET (Reword standard statement to include more specifically what you want students to learn during this lesson):

INTEGRATION WITH F2F SESSIONS (Describe how the online activities will integrate with activities in the F2F sessions):

OPENING TEXT (HOOK) (Include a text of some kind that the students will read or view that "primes the pump"):

ACTIVITY (Describe the activity that the students do in reaction to the text):

POST-ACTIVITY (Describe the reflection activity that the students will do upon completion of the activity):

ASSESSMENT (Describe the assessment that the students will do that will demonstrate learning):

☐ **Make sure group norms have been established.** That includes your own responsiveness and flexibility as you listen to what your students are telling you.

References

Afflerbach, P., & Johnston, P. (1984). Research methodology on the use of verbal reports in reading research. *Journal of Reading Behavior, 16*(4), 307–322.

Applebee, A. N., & Langer, J. A. (2013). *Writing instruction that works: Proven methods for middle and high school classrooms.* New York: Teachers College Press.

Beach, R., Anson, C. M., Breuch, L. K., & Reynolds, T. (2014). *Understanding and creating digital texts: An activity-based approach.* Lanham, MD: Rowman & Littlefield.

Kist, W. (2010). *The socially networked classroom: Teaching in the new media age.* Thousand Oaks, CA: Corwin.

McKeown, R. G., & Gentilucci, J. L. (2007). Think-aloud strategy: Metacognitive development and monitoring comprehension in the middle school second-language classroom. *Journal of Adolescent and Adult Literacy, 51*(2), 136–147.

Pew Research Center. (2015, January 9). Social media update 2014. Retrieved from http://www.pewinternet.org/2015/01/09/social-media-update-2014/

Pytash, K., Batchelor, K., Kist, W., & Srsen, K. (2014). Linked text sets in the English classroom. *The ALAN Review, 42*(1), 52–62.

Sheehy, K. (2012, October 24). States, districts require online ed for high school graduation. *U.S. News and World Report.* Retrieved from http://www.usnews.com/education/blogs/high-school-notes/2012/10/24/states-districts-require-online-ed-for-high-school-graduation

Silberman, M. L. (1996). A*ctive learning: 101 strategies to teach any subject.* Boston: Allyn & Bacon.

Smith, D. F. (2014, November 26). 7 telling statistics about the state of K–12 online learning. *EdTech: Focus on K-12.* Retrieved from http://www.edtechmagazine.com/k12/article/2014/11/7-telling-statistics-about-state-k-12-online-learning

Wiggins, G., & McTighe, J. (2005). *Understanding by design* (2nd ed.). Alexandria, VA: ASCD.

Related ASCD Resources

At the time of publication, the following ASCD resources were available (ASCD stock numbers appear in parentheses). For up-to-date information about ASCD resources, go to www.ascd.org. You can search the complete archives of *Educational Leadership* at www.ascd.org/el.

ASCD EDge®
Exchange ideas and connect with other educators interested in various topics, including blended learning, on the social networking site ASCD EDge at http://ascdedge.ascd.org.

Print Products
Digital Learning Strategies: How Do I Assign and Assess 21st Century Work? (ASCD Arias) by Michael Fisher (#SF114045)

Teaching with Tablets: How Do I Integrate Tablets with Effective Instruction? (ASCD Arias) by Nancy Frey, Doug Fisher, and Alex Gonzalez (#SF113074)

Using Technology with Classroom Instruction That Works, 2nd edition by Howard Pitler, Elizabeth R. Hubbell, and Matt Kuhn (#112012)

ASCD PD Online® Courses
Blended Learning: An Introduction (#PD14OC009)

Technology in Schools: A Balanced Perspective, 2nd edition (#PD11OC109)

For more information: send e-mail to member@ascd.org; call 1-800-933-2723 or 703-578-9600, press 2; send a fax to 703-575-5400; or write to Information Services, ASCD, 1703 N. Beauregard St., Alexandria, VA 22311-1714 USA.

About the Author

William Kist is a professor of Teaching, Learning, and Curriculum Studies at Kent State University, where he teaches literacy courses at the undergraduate and graduate levels. Bill also teaches in the English Department. A former high school English teacher, Bill has spent more than 15 years researching the impact that technology is having on the reading and writing process. The author of *New Literacies in Action*, *The Socially Networked Classroom*, and *The Global School*, Bill has presented nationally and internationally with more than 50 articles and book chapters to his credit. He keeps active as a musician, with a regional Emmy nomination, and can be found online at www.williamkist.com and at https://twitter.com/williamkist.